MONUMENTAL MILESTONES
GREAT EVENTS OF MODERN TIMES

The Story of the Great Depression

The shadow of the Great Depression fell on people of all ages.

Mitchell Lane
PUBLISHERS

P.O. Box 196
Hockessin, Delaware 19707

Titles in the Series

MONUMENTAL MILESTONES
GREAT EVENTS OF MODERN TIMES

The Story of the Great Depression

The shadow of the Great Depression fell on people of all ages.

Mona Gedney

RAP 81/947)

Printing   2   3   4   5   6   7   8   9

    Library of Congress Cataloging-in-Publication Data
Gedney, Mona K.
    The story of the Great Depression / by Mona Gedney.
        p. cm. — (Monumental milestones)
    Includes bibliographical references and index.
    ISBN 1-58415-403-9 (lib. bdg.)
1. United States—History—1933–1945—Juvenile literature. 2. United States—History—1919-1933—Juvenile literature. 3. Depressions—1929—United States—Juvenile literature. 4. New Deal, 1933-1939—Juvenile Literature. 5. United States—Economic conditions—1918-1945—Juvenile literature. I. Title. II. Series.
E806.G44 2005
330.973'0917—dc22   2004024610

ISBN-13: 9781584154037

ABOUT THE AUTHOR: Mona Gedney has been a teacher for thirty-three years and has published sixteen books and numerous short stories. She has a deep-rooted interest in people and places, and her own reading includes essays, history, biography, and travel, as well as fiction, particularly mysteries. She lives in West Lafayette, Indiana.

PHOTO CREDITS: Cover, pp. 1, 3 Library of Congress; p. 6 Getty Images; pp. 12, 14, 16, 22 Library of Congress; p. 28 Corbis; pp. 34, 38 Library of Congress; p. 40 Corbis.

PUBLISHER'S NOTE: This story is based on the author's extensive research, which she believes to be accurate. Documentation of such research is contained on page 46.

The internet sites referenced herein were active as of the publication date. Due to the fleeting nature of some web sites, we cannot guarantee they will all be active when you are reading this book.

PLB2,4

Contents

The Story of the Great Depression

Mona Gedney

*For Your Information

Countless people who had never needed help before were forced to accept the charity of others during the Great Depression.

In 1930, the sister of United States Vice President Charles Curtis was among those helping at a soup kitchen run by the Salvation Army.

The Shadow Falls

In cities and towns all over the United States, food lines stretched for blocks down the streets. Men in business suits, scrubbed schoolchildren, housewives in neatly pressed dresses, and sometimes even youngsters barely able to walk waited grimly. Hoboes in tattered clothes might be standing next to them. They were all there for the same thing. They were waiting for the free handout of bread or soup that would feed them for the day.

By 1932, charity was no longer just for the unfortunate few who had fallen on hard times. Millions of middle-class workers were also out of work. For the first time in their lives, they had to depend upon the generosity of others to feed themselves and their families. Sometimes their desperation was so great that it led to lawlessness. Stories of mobs of people who took food from grocery store shelves while the owners watched helplessly came from states as far apart as Oklahoma and Minnesota.[1] The Great Depression had fallen upon the United States and the world like a dark shadow.

About one-third of the country's work force was unemployed. More than 12 million Americans had lost their jobs and the number was still rising. During the previous three years, national income had fallen by more than 50 percent, from $87.5 billion to $41.7 billion.[2] Thousands of banks across the country had failed.

Thousands of factories and businesses had closed their doors or decreased their work force. Many cities could no longer afford to keep their schools open for a full school year. Sometimes they could not afford to keep them open at all. Millions of children were no longer in school. Many of them had to go to work to help their families survive.[3]

People who had been teachers, secretaries, and shopkeepers just months earlier were walking the streets, looking desperately for jobs that did not exist. Some were standing on city street corners, trying to peddle apples from the Northwest. They often carried a sign encouraging passersby to help them because they were unemployed. Appropriately, one of the year's most popular songs was "Brother, Can You Spare a Dime?"

Many people hoped to find work in some other part of the country. Because they had no money, they hitchhiked or hopped into boxcars and rode the trains illegally. In 1932, the Southern Pacific Railroad alone removed more than 650,000 trespassers from their trains and rail yards. Officials estimated that at least 200,000 of them were teenagers.[4]

In cities all over the country, shantytowns sprang up as the homeless provided for themselves. Their huts were patched together from packing boxes and pieces of wood and whatever other scraps of materials they could find. These sad villages were called "Hoovervilles" because many people blamed President Herbert Hoover for the economic troubles of the country. Nevertheless, having a hut the size of a chicken coop was still better than having nothing at all. In the fall of 1931, the Chicago Commissioner of Public Welfare reported that at least 200 homeless women were sleeping in just two of the city's lakeside parks. The situation was

grim. Winter was approaching and Chicago could provide free overnight lodging for only 100 women.[5]

This desperation was not confined to the cities and towns. Life was little better for many of the country's farmers. Farm prices had fallen drastically, more than 30 percent during the first two years of the Depression. A drought began in 1930, which further aggravated the unhappy situation. It was to continue for several years, creating the infamous "Dust Bowl." Large portions of the Great Plains states quite literally dried up and blew away in choking dust storms.

Countless numbers of farms were put up for auction, leaving the families homeless and hopeless. Some of them headed west for California, where the Depression had not yet had such terrible effects. Some farmers, however, took more aggressive steps. Groups like the Farmers' Holiday Association prevented produce from being taken to market in cities across the Midwest. They demanded higher prices for their goods. They turned back trucks trying to enter the cities. In some places the National Guard was called out to disperse them. Edward O'Neal of the American Farm Bureau Federation warned that the country could be facing a revolution if nothing was done to improve the plight of the farmers. His words echoed a similar warning from the president of the American Federation of Labor, who maintained that open revolution might result if men and women could find no work in spite of their best efforts.

In the spring of 1932, a protest movement began in Oregon. Its leaders were veterans of World War I, many of them now unemployed. In 1924, Congress had passed a "bonus bill" that promised war veterans a cash bonus for their service. It was in the form of bonds that would be ready for payment in 1945. Because of

their desperation, the veterans felt that the bonus should be paid immediately. The group decided they would journey to Washington, D.C., to make their feelings on the subject known.

By the time they reached Washington, veterans from every state in the country had joined them. Up to 20,000 men camped in shanties near the Capitol Building, waiting to hear what action Congress would take. During World War I, they had been called the American Expeditionary Force. Now they dubbed themselves the BEF, the Bonus Expeditionary Force.

The House was intimidated by the presence of so many dissatisfied veterans. It passed the Bonus Bill, which called for the bonus to be paid at once. The Senate, however, decided that passing it would be giving in to mob violence. When the news of the bill's defeat was announced to the men waiting outside the Capitol, they were unhappy, but there was no violence. Congress adjourned and many of the men left Washington. Nonetheless, many members of the government were worried about having the BEF camped on their doorstep. The Russian Revolution had occurred only 15 years earlier. Some feared a similar revolution was possible in this country.

At the end of July, some of the veterans had an encounter with the police. One veteran was killed and several on both sides were injured. The government sent federal troops to drive the unarmed veterans, some of whom were accompanied by their families, from their camp. They were given an hour to pack their possessions and then tear gas was used. Later investigations revealed that there was no threat of revolution from the BEF.[6]

The veterans, like so many of their countrymen, faced a dim future. The year was 1932. The Great Depression, which had it's official beginning in 1929, was three years old. It would continue until 1941.

Even during the Depression—or perhaps *because* of the Depression—people were eager for entertainment. They wanted an escape from the grimness of everyday life.

During 1932, 60 million Americans attended the movies weekly. Adults usually paid 15 cents and children a dime. They watched westerns and mysteries, adventures, and comedies. Popular movies had little to do

Young Adults Listening to the Radio

with the troubles people were facing in their daily lives, so they offered at least a short holiday.

The radio provided hours of entertainment. People could listen to music, comedies, soap operas, dramas, variety shows, news, and farm reports. Families gathered around the radio to enjoy their programs together. Despite the economic problems, more than two-thirds of American households owned a radio by 1940.

People still enjoyed sports. Baseball was the great American pastime. In 1932, Babe Ruth remained a national figure, and everyone knew about the New York Yankees, the Chicago Cubs, and the other major league teams. A sport of a different kind became popular during the 1930s. Thousands of miniature golf courses sprang up around the country. At just 15 cents a game, it became the rage.

At home, families played the board game Monopoly, as well as old favorites such as checkers and chess. Card playing increased, and the sale of decks of cards spiked during 1931. Bridge was particularly popular. Younger players as well as adults enjoyed it.

Possibly the oddest form of entertainment was the dance marathon, a craze that began during the 1920s. It was inexpensive, and the dancers received several meals each day, a very real benefit during those hungry times. They also had the chance to win a cash prize if they could stay on their feet long enough. Often the marathons lasted several weeks and even longer. One in Chicago was said to have lasted for nine months. A few hardy dancers managed to last and to win the cash prize at the end.

By 1935, the dance marathon craze was fading, but other pastimes were growing in popularity. Weary or not, broke or not, the American public still wanted entertainment.

FARM
TO WIN
"OverThere"

President Woodrow Wilson guided through World War I.

He worked ardently to establish the League of Nations, which the United States refused to join. In 1919, President Wilson was awarded the 1919 Nobel Peace Prize for his efforts to establish the League of Nations at the close of the war.

How It All Began

No one can be absolutely certain why the Great Depression occurred. Many books have been written about it, and experts have expressed a variety of opinions. Most certainly, the Depression did not occur because of a single event. Many people think that the stock market crash of 1929 caused the Depression, but the answer is not that simple. The crash was the most visible and the most dramatic cause, but it was by no means the only one.

In the first decades of the twentieth century, a series of earth-shaking events changed the world in which Americans lived. Because the changes were so drastic, the people—even the country's leaders—were not certain what to expect in the future. World War I changed America's place in world society. Economic relationships with other countries shifted. Rapid growth in technology increased the production of goods in America and other countries. However, the markets for those goods were also changing. People were trying to decide how to deal with those changes. Also, attitudes were different after the war. Many people wanted to enjoy their lives now, rather than saving up and waiting to have their good times later. All of these changes played a part in bringing about the Great Depression.

World War I created a new set of problems for the United States. Before the war, the United States believed strongly in isolationism.[1] After it was over, the government wished to return to that policy. President Woodrow Wilson proposed that the United States should join the newly formed League of Nations. The design of the League was similar to the modern-day United Nations. Although many people supported the idea, Congress rejected it. The country decided to return to what President Warren G. Harding—who succeeded Wilson—called "normalcy." In other words, people wanted life to be as much as possible like it had been before World War I.

Herbert Hoover served as President of the United States from 1929 to 1933.

Many people blamed President Hoover for the loss of their jobs and homes, and the shantytowns that sprang up around the country were called "Hoovervilles."

That, however, proved to be impossible. Too many things had changed. The United States had become a major world power. Up until that time, Great Britain had been the leader of the world economy. The British had helped to keep that economy on an even keel. They had policies that encouraged lending money to other countries when times were bad and spending it at home when times were good. The United States, like most countries, was mainly interested in taking care of its own economy after the war. It was not particularly interested in the economies of other countries. What most governments failed to realize was how greatly their economies now affected one another.

After the war, the United States wished to sell as many of its products as possible to the rest of the world. However, it did not want to buy very much from other countries. The U.S. placed high tariffs on products from other countries. That was done to encourage the sale of goods produced in the United States. Also, American investors tended to lend their money internationally when times were good. When times were bad, they invested at home. This practice did not help to make the world economy more stable.[2]

Another important factor was that the economies of many countries were already weak because of debts caused by the war. During the 1920s, some Americans chose to invest large amounts of money in European countries. They lent those countries money to repay their war debts and earned a very good rate of interest on their investments. This also meant that the American economy became more closely connected to the economies of other countries.

Adolph Treidler created this poster for the U.S. Department of Labor.

Posters like this one appealed to farmers to help with the war effort "Over There" in Europe. Many farmers did increase their acreage to produce more crops during World War I, but the end of the war caused their market to decrease.

American farmers began having problems very soon after the war ended. During the war years of 1914-1918, they supplied Europe with much of its agricultural produce. The war was fought across European lands, so farmers there could not raise their normal crops. During those years, American farmers increased their acreage by about 40 percent. As they increased the size of their farms, they also increased their debt. Between 1910 and 1920, farm mortgages doubled.

When the war was over, European farmers once again raised and marketed their own crops. The demand for American agricultural products decreased. Unfortunately, American farmers still had their debts to pay. Now, however, they did not have enough

paying markets. To add to their problems, the use of automobiles and tractors increased at this time, replacing horses and mules. That eliminated the need to feed those animals, which further cut down on farm income. Long before the Great Depression arrived, life for many farmers was unstable. Their average annual income was less than half that of most other Americans.

Factories and businesses had become increasingly industrialized, so they produced more goods and they produced them faster. However, there were not enough people who were able to buy many of these goods. The answer was the installment plan. Now people could buy things on credit, paying a little of the total cost every month.

For many people, life during the 1920s was about trying to get rich—or richer—as quickly and as easily as possible. It was an optimistic time. Everything seemed possible. Only a few years ago there had been no automobiles, refrigerators, or radios! The world was changing, and there were fortunes to be made. For many Americans, the stock market seemed to offer the best chance for making a fortune quickly.

Many people bought stocks on margin. In other words, they paid just a part of the price, sometimes as little as 10 percent. Then they used that stock as collateral for a loan for the rest of the amount. If the stock rose in value—as most stocks did during that period—they could sell it quickly. The money that they made let them repay the loan and make a profit, too.

Many foreign investors also decided that buying stocks on margin was a good use of their money. Wall Street became very attractive to people around the world with money to invest. Large

American corporations, which were making a great deal of profit because of increased productions and lower costs, invested their money, too. They could have used some of that money to increase workers' wages, but they decided to use it to make still more money. Banks, too, invested their customers' money in these profitable ventures. Few rules governed the way in which the stock market or the banks were run. It may have seemed to some people that this system of steady profits could go on forever.

Then came Black Tuesday.

That was October 29, 1929, the usual date given for the stock market crash. On that single day, the stock market lost fifteen billion dollars. However, the market had become unstable early in September, and the crash actually stretched over ten long weeks. Many investors—both large and small—were wiped out. And stock prices kept falling. And falling. The decline finally stopped in July, 1932. Its effects would linger far longer.

Much of the buying power of America belonged to the people, corporations, and banks that had just lost their money in the stock crash. They had been damaged and they had lost their confidence in the system. Over the next months, production of goods slowed because there was less demand for them. As this happened, factories and businesses cut back on the number of workers they employed. Because of this, there was even less money available for spending.

Banks that had lost their investments called in loans they had made to their customers. If the customers could not repay the loans, they lost their houses or their cars or whatever else they had offered the bank as collateral. Often that wasn't enough for

the banks to survive. In the three years after the stock market crash, several thousand banks were forced to close. People who had kept their accounts in those banks simply lost their money. Disasters like these caused many people to remove their money from their bank accounts and keep it at home. This took large amounts of money out of circulation, which increased the financial problems of the country.

In 1930, Congress passed the Hawley-Smoot Tariff Act. It was supposed to protect American farmers and businesses. However, it actually raised the prices of goods they needed. It also created problems for countries that exported their goods to the United States. They could not earn enough money from their sales to repay the debts their countries owed. Some of those debts, of course, were owed to investors in the United States. Banks and businesses in other countries began to fail, too. The shadow of the Depression stretched across most of the world.

Like many people, President Hoover believed strongly that the U.S. government should not interfere with the economy. After the stock market crash, he met with business leaders and encouraged them to keep their workers employed and not to reduce wages. However, he was not willing for the government to tell businesses what to do. He believed the problems of the economy would work themselves out. The country had faced other depressions in the past and had weathered them. It was, he thought, simply a matter of enduring the problem until it passed. Others thought so, too. Plans to erect the Empire State Building were announced just six weeks before Black Tuesday, and its builders insisted that its construction continue on schedule.

Unfortunately, the Great Depression was proving to be longer and more deeply rooted than earlier depressions. The economy showed no sign of improvement, and many offices in the new Empire State Building stood empty. Finally, in 1932, President Hoover established the Reconstruction Finance Corporation to lend money to banks. The RFC did not work out well, however, and little was accomplished.

President Hoover also believed that individuals should depend on themselves. If they did have a problem, private charities were there to offer help. However, as more and more people lost their jobs and their homes, local charities could no longer help them all. States that offered relief for unemployment ran out of money. Still, the president did not believe that the job of the government was to offer help to the unemployed. Many unemployed people agreed with him. They were deeply ashamed of their failure to find work. Not everyone agreed, however. The shantytowns that sheltered the homeless were named "Hoovervilles." This showed many people blamed President Hoover for the problems they were facing.

As the desperate year of 1932 drew to a close, the November election brought a resounding victory for the Democratic Party. The new president, whose campaign song was "Happy Days Are Here Again," was Franklin Delano Roosevelt. When he had accepted his party's nomination, he had made a promise, saying, "I pledge you, I pledge myself, to a new deal for the American people!"[3]

The American people had shown with their votes that they were ready for the new deal that Roosevelt promised.

On May 1, 1931, the Empire State Building took its place on Fifth Avenue in New York City as a symbol of American life and confidence for the future. Some people called it "the eighth wonder of the world." At that time, it was the tallest building in the world, reaching 1250 feet to the tip of its lightning rod. It was 204 feet higher than the Chrysler Building, which had held the title until that time, and more than 250 feet higher than France's famed Eiffel Tower.

The Empire State Building

It took only one year and 45 days—or seven million man-hours—to build. Three thousand workers labored steadily to accomplish this feat. They accomplished this miraculous achievement in spite of sixteen design changes during the planning and construction of the building.

Composed of 60,000 tons of steel, the Empire State Building is kept stable by its columns and beams. Even in winds of 110 miles per hour, the building is designed to give no more than half an inch. Its lightning rod absorbs about 100 strikes of lightning each year. In 1945, the building even proved sturdy enough to withstand the impact of a B-25 bomber that lost its way in the fog. The building sustained only minor damage from the crash.

At the time of the construction, it was anticipated that many people would soon be traveling in passenger dirigibles. Therefore, a mooring mast for these dirigibles was erected at the top of the building to provide the convenience of arriving in the middle of the city. That, of course, never came to be because dirigibles did not prove to be a practical form of transportation.

More recent skyscrapers, like the Sears Tower in Chicago and the Petronas Towers in Kuala Lumpur, Malaysia, have surpassed the Empire State Building in height. None, however, have surpassed it in appeal. It remains a famous personality in its own right, appearing in movies, television shows, and countless posters and photographs. It is still a well-known symbol of American confidence and efficiency.

Franklin Delano Roosevelt served as the president through two great crises of century.

These two great crises were the Great Depression and World War II. President Franklin Delano Roosevelt had begun serving his fourth term as president when he died on April 12, 1945.

CHAPTER 3

The New Deal

During the time between the November election and Roosevelt's inauguration on March 4 the following year, the economic situation of the country grew even worse. The number of unemployed continued to increase. So many banks had closed that it appeared the nation's financial system would soon collapse. Even large banks in New York and Chicago were closing their doors. Business was coming to a standstill. In his inaugural address, President Roosevelt assured the country "that the only thing we have to fear is fear itself."[1] It appeared to most Americans that there was much to fear.

The new president took immediate steps to deal with this fear. He used his presidential powers to announce a national "bank holiday" starting on March 6. All the country's banks would be closed. So would the New York Stock Exchange. He then called a special session of Congress. During the four days before the session met, a group of experts that included both Democrats and Republicans worked frantically to design a program that would save the banking system. The bill that they prepared—the Emergency Banking Act—was passed almost immediately by the House. It was rushed to the Senate, where it was also passed at once. The president signed it into law that night. The members of

Congress overwhelmingly supported the measures he had taken to control the banking crisis.

That Sunday night—March 12—he gave the first of his now famous "fireside chats." It was a radio address to the nation, but it was not a stiff, formal speech. He wanted listeners to feel that they were sitting with him at a fireside, talking over important matters in the way that friends would.

His subject was banking. He explained in simple terms what the problems with the banks were and what the government was doing to solve them. He announced that some banks would reopen the next day. Those that reopened had been carefully checked and pronounced safe. People could use them without fear. Other banks would take more work, he told them. They would not be allowed to open until they too were safe.

He did not sugarcoat the message. He said that he could not promise that all banks would reopen. Nor could he promise that some people would not still lose the money they had placed in those banks. He assured them, though, that once a bank did reopen, they could trust it and keep their money in it safely. He told them that the most important thing that the banking system could have was the confidence of the people. He ended his talk with a direct appeal to his listeners, saying: "It is your problem no less than it is mine. Together we cannot fail."[2]

His listeners believed him. The next morning, some of the banks reopened as promised. There were withdrawals of money, but there were also deposits. In fact, more money was deposited than withdrawn. That was a very encouraging sign. By the end of the month, 75 percent of the banks had reopened. Roosevelt's ability to communicate his ideas in a convincing manner was one of the

key elements of his success as a president. He had shown that in his first fireside chat.

The Emergency Banking Act was the first of an amazing number of bills that Congress passed in that special session, which became known as the Hundred Days. Reading about the programs established during this period is much like swimming through alphabet soup because of the abbreviations by which they quickly became known. For instance, the Civilian Conservation Corps was called the CCC, the Federal Emergency Relief Administration was the FERA, and the National Recovery Administration was the NRA.

The CCC (Civilian Conservation Corps) was a special project designed by President Roosevelt. He wanted to help people and he was very interested in conservation. The program recruited unemployed young men to work on projects in the national forests and national parks. They were housed and fed and paid a small salary. By 1935, the CCC employed 500,000 men. Some of them were the veterans from the BEF (Bonus Expeditionary Force). They worked on a variety of projects, from building roads and trails to planting trees and conducting wildlife surveys.

The FERA (Federal Emergency Relief Administration) was also designed to help people. Charities did not have enough money to help the large number of people in need. Also, people did not simply want charity; they wanted jobs. The federal administration provided funds to state FERA offices. These offices were responsible for planning projects within their states and using the funds to employ local people to work on those projects. The offices were also supposed to raise additional state money for relief of their citizens. Later in 1933, the CWA (Civil Works Administration) was established as a temporary part of FERA. Its purpose was to help

people through the winter of 1933-34 by providing jobs working on public projects like the repair and building of schools, bridges, and highways. At one time during that winter, the CWA employed four million people.

The NRA (National Recovery Administration) was created by the National Industrial Recovery Act. The NRA was designed to work with industries and their labor forces to reform businesses. Its objective was to provide industrial employment for millions and to help the economy. Businesses were asked to establish a shorter working week, which would allow them to hire more workers, and to pay their workers a salary they could live on. At the same time, businesses were asked to agree not to immediately raise the prices of the goods they were producing. President Roosevelt felt that having a large number of people employed would mean that businesses would sell more of their products. That would, for the moment, provide a profit for the businesses.

Trade associations (groups of businesses that produced the same kinds of items) were asked to cooperate with one another and to write codes that would regulate their businesses. These would do such things as set prices and salaries and working hours that all businesses would agree to use. Needless to say, problems arose immediately because not everyone wished to cooperate. The NRA lasted only two years before the Supreme Court declared that it was unconstitutional. Perhaps the most important thing the NRA accomplished was promoting the idea of cooperation between government and business.

The National Industrial Recovery Act itself (which had come to be known simply as the NRA) did help to control child labor. It also introduced the idea of a minimum wage and a maximum number

of hours for a work week. President Roosevelt said that the act gave workers "a new charter of rights long sought and hitherto denied."[3] Workers were allowed the right to join unions, to bargain for wage increases, and to strike. These rights were of great importance to workers and led to the rise of labor unions during the 1930s. When the NRA was struck down by the Supreme Court, the establishment of the National Labor Relations Board protected workers' rights.

Some historians believe that the most effective part of the National Industrial Recovery Act was the Public Works Administration (PWA). Like the CCC and CWA, the PWA established projects that provided jobs. The projects for the PWA were carefully planned and employed skilled workers, such as architects and engineers. One of their major projects was the completion of Boulder Dam. Construction of the dam, which had begun in 1930 during the Hoover Administration, was accelerated. It was finished in 1935, two years ahead of the original schedule.

President Roosevelt ended his first talk to the public about the National Industrial Recovery Act with these hopeful words: "Between these twin efforts—public works and industrial reemployment—it is not too much to expect that a great many men and women can be taken from the ranks of the unemployed before winter comes. It is the most important attempt of this kind in history. As in the great crisis of the World War, it puts a whole people to the simple but vital test: 'Must we go on in many groping, disorganized, separate units to defeat or shall we move as one great team to victory?' "[4]

The establishment of the Tennessee Valley Authority (TVA) was another important accomplishment. The TVA built dams in a

The Norris Dam in Chattanooga, Tennessee, was completed in 1936. It was the first dam built by the Tennessee Valley Authority.

Dams like this one brought electricity—and progress—to the Tennessee Valley.

seven-state area to provide flood control and electricity. Farms that had not had access to electricity would now have it. Electricity could also be used to industrialize the Tennessee Valley. In addition, the TVA set up programs to teach the people how to make the most of their land.

The Hundred Days produced other important legislation. Some of it helped farmers, some helped homeowners, some regulated the banking system.

A feeling of cautious optimism appeared in the country during the Hundred Days and the months that followed. The Depression

was still a part of life, but now more people had jobs. They could see that the government had been very busy in an attempt to solve the country's problems. People allowed themselves to hope, but the shadow of the Depression still lingered. In fact, throughout the 1930s, the economy remained a serious problem. Still, the country's situation was never quite as grim again as it had been in 1932 and the winter of 1933 when the financial system was about to collapse and hope seemed very far away.

Solving the economic problems of the nation was a huge task. President Roosevelt was doing his best to restore confidence, and, to a large extent, he had done so. A great deal of the legislation that was passed during the Hundred Days and in the remainder of his first term of office helped the situation. Some did not.

The president was not afraid of failure. He kept trying to find solutions. His New Deal program, he said, consisted of reform, relief, and recovery. Relief was just that—an effort to provide immediate relief to as many of the unemployed as possible to help bring about the recovery of the country's economy. Reform took longer. It meant passing laws to keep the same problems from occurring again. One of those laws was the Securities and Exchange Commission Act, which President Roosevelt signed in June, 1934. It established a commission to regulate the American stock market and to protect investors from dishonest practices. In the same year, Congress passed an act that established the Federal Deposit Insurance Corporation (FDIC). Through the FDIC, the federal government insured an individual's deposit in a bank up to $10,000.

In 1935, President Roosevelt pressed for a new wave of legislation. Some historians call it the Second New Deal. The passage of the Emergency Relief Appropriations Act allowed him

to establish the Works Progress Administration (WPA). This was yet another agency to provide work for the unemployed. Although it did provide work (at very low wages) and it did provide services for the country, five million people were still without work. Nevertheless, countless projects were completed.

Among them were artistic programs. The WPA established the Federal Writers' Project, the Federal Music Project, the Federal Art Project, and the Federal Theatre Project. Artistic people used their particular talents to benefit the public. The writers produced a vast quantity of material, including colorful and interesting guides to all the states and collections of folklore. Among the activities of the Music Project were organizing orchestras, presenting concerts, giving free music lessons to the public, and collecting American folk music. Those in the Art Project painted murals in public buildings across the country, created sculptures, offered free art lessons to the public, and, in general, attempted to provide "art for the millions." The Theatre Project tried to accomplish the same goal by presenting plays, puppet shows, and dance productions to people who had never had the opportunity to attend the theater. Not everyone approved of these projects, however. Some called them propaganda for the New Deal. The Theatre Project was cut in 1939, but the others continued until 1943.

In 1935, Congress also passed the Social Security Act. It provided pensions for the elderly, the unemployed, the handicapped, and dependent mothers and children. Many European countries already had such pensions, which were paid for by the government. In the U.S., however, they were paid for by taxes on the workers' income and the employers' payrolls. Like many other New Deal programs, Social Security met with great opposition from those who

felt that the government should not be so involved in the lives of people.

Nevertheless, Franklin Roosevelt was elected to a second term of office in 1936. The following year, the country suffered a definite pause in its recovery, which the president's enemies happily referred to as "Roosevelt's recession."[5] The president had decided to limit government spending. He cut the number of people employed by the WPA in half. Also, Social Security payments were being collected from paychecks and from employers, which meant that two billion dollars was not being used for purchasing items. Leaders of industry were nervous about the New Deal and its effects on their profits, so they were not spending money to expand their businesses.

The combined effects were unfortunate. Once again the number of unemployed rose, and hunger became a very real problem. Once again charities—and this time state relief agencies —were running out of money. Finally the president gave in and asked Congress for almost four billion dollars to be divided among relief agencies like the WPA and the PWA. Once again, the country began to recover.

The Fair Labor Standards Act, the final major piece of legislation of the New Deal, was passed in April, 1938. Many fought bitterly against it, and some changes were made before it was passed. It still provided for a 44-hour work week and a minimum wage of 25 cents per hour. Within two years the work week would be reduced to 40 hours and the minimum wage would rise to 40 cents an hour. The Fair Labor Standards Act also outlawed the use of child labor in interstate commerce.

By 1939, the power of the president was decreasing. Many people still disagreed with the New Deal and feared the power that Roosevelt had gained. "Roosevelt's recession" resulted in a number of Republicans gaining state governorships and seats in Congress following the 1938 elections. Also, ten years had passed since the stock market crash, yet the number of unemployed remained large. It had begun to seem that the United States would always have a large number of unemployed workers. People were discouraged, and they had grown tired.

By now, it had also begun to dawn on Americans that there was trouble brewing in other parts of the world. Spain had suffered a civil war. Japan was at war with China. Italy had invaded Ethiopia. Hitler and his Nazi Party had gained power in Germany. In 1938 Hitler annexed neighboring Austria. Later that year he took over the Sudetenland, a major part of Czechoslovakia. While America's Neutrality Act had prevented any action on the part of the government, the U.S. ambassador to Germany was recalled late that year.

Strangely enough, it was these distant troubles that would finally deliver the United States from the shadow of the Great Depression.

A Black Blizzard

Several years of drought that began in 1930 eventually took a heavy toll on the southern plains. The area that was affected became known as the "Dust Bowl." One result was huge dust storms that presented people with a life and death problem. These "black blizzards," fearful dark clouds of dust rolling across the landscape, swallowed everything in darkness as they passed. Everything in their wake was left covered with inches of dust. Aside from ruining crops and the land used for farming and grazing, the storms were dangerous. They damaged the lungs and eyes, causing a variety of health problems. Many animals suffocated. The grit ruined the engines of cars and tractors.

The drought was not the only cause of the dust storms. During the years of World War I, wheat and other crops were needed. More land was plowed and planted. After the war, some people tried to industrialize farming. Still more land was placed under cultivation. Allowing cattle and sheep to overgraze pasture land, leaving little grass behind, added to the problem. The result was grim. The grass had held the dirt in place. Now a strong wind could pick up tons of good soil and simply blow it away. This came to the immediate attention of those in Washington, D.C., when a storm in 1934 carried dust hundreds of miles to the White House.

In 1933, the federal government created the Soil Erosion Service and in 1934 the Grazing Service to try to control the problem. During those same years, the Federal Emergency Relief Administration spent $85 million to buy damaged farmland and to try to restore it. In an effort to prevent wind erosion of the soil, farmers were paid to plant belts of trees and to plow high ridges that provided windbreaks.

The New Deal provided agencies to protect the land—even from its owners. Although there have been other droughts and dust storms, there has fortunately been nothing to equal the Dust Bowl.

The bombing of Pearl Harbor caused the to enter World War II, and it was the w to restore the economy.

The USS West Virginia was one of the battleships struck during the attack.

The End of the Great Depression

In spite of the efforts of Franklin Roosevelt and the federal government, it was not the New Deal that finally put an end to the Great Depression. It was war. England and France, watching Hitler's activities in Europe, realized that they probably would soon have to go to war with Germany. As part of their preparations, they began to stockpile food so they would have enough on hand if and when the war began. They bought much of it from the United States. Early in 1939, President Roosevelt asked Congress for a large increase in the defense budget. If there was to be a war, the U.S. must be ready, Roosevelt explained. This extra money would be poured into American companies and would help revitalize the economy.

Germany invaded Poland in September, 1939. England and France immediately declared war. President Roosevelt began a serious military buildup early the following year. He asked Congress for much more money. The country was not yet at war, but the possibility was becoming more likely. Thousands of aircraft, ships, and tanks had to be built. So did new factories. More workers had to be hired. The U.S. armed forces had to be increased. Roosevelt was elected to a third term in 1940. He proposed an even larger

defense budget in 1941. By the middle of that year, the economy was healthier than it had been in twenty years.

In 1933, a British economist named John Maynard Keynes had written an open letter to President Roosevelt that was published in the *New York Times*. In the letter, he gave his advice about the most important thing to help the economy recover. He believed that government spending financed by loans was the answer. Keynes pointed out that war was usually considered "the only legitimate excuse for creating employment by government expenditure."[1]

What Keynes was proposing is called deficit spending, using borrowed money to cover expenditures. During the 1930s, Roosevelt tried to avoid deficit spending whenever he could. The New Deal and its programs had been expensive, but not nearly as expensive as they could have been.

Now, however, with war looming on the horizon, he had no choice. He had to borrow huge sums of money to revitalize the military and prepare the country for war. All this money that was poured into the nation's defense created hundreds of thousands of jobs. It brought complete recovery to the economy.

On December 7, 1941, the Great Depression came to an end when the Japanese bombed Pearl Harbor. The United States entered World War II and established a wartime economy for the next four years. Millions of Americans entered the armed services. At home many factories operated around the clock to provide everything needed for the war effort. The prosperity that people had been looking for since 1929 had finally arrived—at the price of a war.

On Sunday, December 7, 1941, the U.S. Pacific fleet stationed at Pearl Harbor in the Hawaiian Islands was struck without warning by Japanese bombers and torpedo planes. By the end of the attack, six military sites on Oahu had been hit, 21 American ships had been damaged or destroyed, and more than 320 American aircraft had been destroyed. The American death toll was 2,390. On the USS *Arizona* alone, 1,177 lives were lost when it suffered a direct hit, erupted in flames, and sank within minutes.[1]

Ship Wreckage after the Attack on Pearl Harbor

In his speech to Congress and the nation on December 8, President Roosevelt described the attack on Pearl Harbor, as well as the subsequent attacks on Guam, Wake Island, the Philippine Islands, and Midway Island. He began the speech by referring to December 7, 1941, with the now famous phrase, "a date which will live in infamy." And at its close, he called upon Congress to declare that a state of war had existed between the United States and Japan from the time of "the unprovoked and dastardly attack." He signed the declaration of war on the same day. Soon the United States was also at war with Germany and Italy, both allies of Japan.

On Tuesday, December 9, President Roosevelt held another "fireside chat" with the nation to discuss the declaration of war on Japan. In it, he referred to the assembly lines producing military equipment that the country had established a year and a half earlier. However, what had been produced was not adequate to fight the war the country was entering. Roosevelt announced that production in the war industry would go on seven days a week, new plants would be built, and old ones increased in size.

War brought hard work and terrible sacrifices—but it also brought the end of the Great Depression.

The shadow of the Depression fell on ages.

When families lost their homes, they often were forced to take shelter in one of the country's many "Hoovervilles."

CHAPTER 5

Why the Great Depression Was Important

There are many reasons why the Great Depression was important. It is a dramatic story from American history, beginning with a stock market crash that marked the end of the Roaring Twenties and ending with a world war. It was a time of suffering and endurance that made many Americans value not only toughness but also justice. Much of the New Deal was about making life better for everyone in the country, not just the wealthy. The Great Depression left a legacy of laws to protect the country from many of the evils that caused it.

The fears of being without a job and of losing their money ran deep in people who lived through the Depression. Even those who were very young then still have vivid memories of that time. Those living in cities remember seeing breadlines, even if they didn't have to stand in them. Those who lived in the country remember the countless hoboes who appeared at their doors. At many homes, particularly those marked with the special hoboes' sign to show that a kind woman lived within, a stranger from the road would often eat supper with the family—or at the very least, receive a handout of food. Seeing the homeless, remembering the

39

Hoovervilles—these are things that still haunt those who lived during those times. Many who did not have much themselves are proud of the fact that they and their families "made do" during the Depression and survived it. The grim time tested the resilience of the American people, but their optimism and determination gave them strength. It was suitable that the theme of the New York World's Fair, which opened in 1939, was "The World of Tomorrow." Americans were once more looking toward the future with hope.

Because of the Great Depression, legislation was passed to try to keep such a thing from happening again. The New Deal provided regulations to keep the banking system stable and insure

President Roosevelt signed into law many measures intended to help stabilize the economy and to help the American people.

During the "Hundred Days" of the special session called in 1933, fifteen major laws and many minor ones were adopted.

those who keep their money in banks. The Securities and Exchange Commission was established to monitor the stock market and to protect investors from dishonest practices. The New Deal also provided Social Security, payments for the unemployed, and welfare payments. The rise of labor unions gave greater power to workers and allowed them to bargain for better wages and working conditions. All of these things help to keep the economy stable.

The presidency of Franklin Delano Roosevelt forever changed the relationship between government and business, as well as the relationship between government and the individual. In a campaign speech on April 7, 1932, before he was first elected president, Roosevelt made a point that was the foundation for all of the New Deal. He said that the present administration "can think in terms only of the top of the social and economic structure. It has sought temporary relief from the top down rather than from the bottom up."[1] Roosevelt said that in order for plans to work effectively, the government must "put their faith once more in the forgotten man at the bottom of the economic pyramid."[2]

The nation was filled with forgotten men—and women—who heard him and believed him. Because of them, he was able to make the government accept some responsibility for the welfare of the people. The changes were made with the belief that every person is of value.

And that may be the most enduring legacy of the Great Depression.

The New York World's Fair opened on April 30, 1939. Its theme was "The World of Tomorrow," and the complete slogan was "Building the World of Tomorrow with the Tools of Today."

A group of businessmen planned the fair, and it was intended to be a technological marvel. It also had exhibits from many different countries to emphasize international cooperation. President Roosevelt opened the fair, and this event was televised. It was the first day of television broadcasting in New York City and made a very suitable beginning for "The World of Tomorrow."

The Perisphere and the Trylon

Much of the design of the fair was modernistic. At the entrance were two huge futuristic symbols. One was a 750-foot-high spike called the Trylon. Next to it was a globe 200 feet in diameter called the Perisphere. Both of them were painted a stark white. The Futurama exhibit at the General Motors pavilion was a huge scale model of America as it would be in 1960. The exhibit included houses, dams, greenbelts, and super highways that would allow speeds of 100 miles per hour. The RCA exhibit included the newest form of communication, the television. Two of the favorites of the fair were at the Westinghouse exhibit: the robot Elektro and his robot dog Sparko.

More than 60 countries had exhibits at the fair, although theirs were cultural rather than technological. The food, art, and dances of each country were presented, much like Disney's Epcot Center does today.

Germany, however, was not represented. It invaded Poland just over four months after the fair opened. By the time the fair closed late the following year, World War II was well underway.

For a brief space, the fair took the people's minds from the Great Depression, which had shadowed their lives for so long and given them a view of the possibilities of the future. In another five years the war would be over, and people could begin building The World of Tomorrow.

Chronology of the Great Depression

1929 Crash of the New York Stock Exchange starts the Great Depression

1930 Congress passes Hawley-Smoot Tariff Act

1932 Franklin Delano Roosevelt defeats Herbert Hoover in the presidential election and promises a "new deal"

1933 The Hundred Days of legislation following Roosevelt's inauguration results in passage of many of his New Deal programs

1934 Congress approves the Securities and Exchange Commission Act

1935 Legislation for the "Second New Deal" includes the Social Security Act; the Supreme Court rules that the NRA is unconstitutional

1936 Roosevelt is elected for a second term

1937 The Fair Labor Standards Act becomes law; "Roosevelt's Recession" begins

1938 Germany annexes Austria; German troops march unopposed into Czechoslovakia

1939 Germany invades Poland, which begins World War II

1940 Roosevelt is elected for a third term

1941 The Japanese attack on Pearl Harbor leads to U.S. involvement in World War II and the end of the Great Depression

Timeline in History

1882   Franklin Delano Roosevelt is born.

1886   The American Federation of Labor is founded.

1892   The Homestead Steel Strike results in a significant loss of power and influence for labor unions.

1907   The Panic of 1907 causes a run on banks.

1913   The 16th Amendment establishes a federal income tax.

1914   The United States enters World War I.

1916   The National Park Service is established.

1918   World War I ends.

1920   The 20th Amendment gives women the right to vote.

1924   Robert Frost's *A Poem with Notes and Grace Notes* wins the Pulitzer Prize.

1925   Adolf Hitler reorganizes the Nazi Party in Germany and becomes its leader.

1931   The Empire State Building is completed and becomes the world's tallest building.

1933   Hitler is given dictatorial powers.

1937   Japan seizes parts of China; Amelia Earhart disappears while flying across the Pacific Ocean.

1944   Franklin D. Roosevelt is elected to a fourth term as president.

1945   Roosevelt dies; World War II ends.

1950   The United States enters the Korean War.

1953   Scientists James Watson and Francis Crick describe the double helix structure of the DNA molecule; the Korean War ends.

1957   The Soviet Union begins the Space Age by launching the first satellite.

1963   President John F. Kennedy is assassinated.

1964   U.S. combat troops are sent to Vietnam.

1968   Civil Rights leader Martin Luther King, Jr., is assassinated.

1969   U.S. astronauts Neil Armstrong and Buzz Aldrin become the first humans to walk on the moon.

1975   The United States leaves Vietnam.

1977   Apple Computers produces the first personal computer.

1981   Sandra Day O'Connor becomes the first woman appointed to the U.S. Supreme Court.

1986   The London stock market is deregulated and many restrictions are removed.

1987   President Ronald Reagan announces the nation's first trillion-dollar budget.

1989   The wall separating East and West Berlin is torn down.

2004   President George W. Bush proposes a $2.4 trillion budget for 2005.

2005   Comptroller General David Walker warns that future generations will not be able to sustain the combination of Social Security, Medicare, and Medicaid unless changes in these programs are made.

Chapter Notes

Chapter 1
The Shadow Falls

1. T. H. Watkins, *The Great Depression: American in the 1930s* (New York: Little, Brown, and Company, 1993), pp. 79-81.

2. Robert Goldston, *The Great Depression* (Indianapolis, Indiana: The Bobbs-Merrill Company, 1968), p. 57.

3. Some children had to work in sweat-shop conditions. A few even died of starvation during this period.

4. T. H. Watkins, *The Great Depression: American in the 1930s* (New York: Little, Brown, and Company, 1993), p. 60.

5. This news was reported in the *New York Times* and was typical of the stories of Hoovervilles and bread lines that were appearing around the country.

6. Robert Goldston, *The Great Depression* (Indianapolis, Indiana: The Bobbs-Merrill Company, 1968) pp. 61-66.

Chapter 2
How It All Began

1. In other words, the United States preferred to remain isolated from other countries. The government was not particularly interested in building relationships with them.

2. Robert S. McElvaine, *The Great Depression* (New York: Times Books, 1984), pp. 33-34.

3. Robert Goldston, *The Great Depression* (Indianapolis, Indiana: The Bobbs-Merrill Company, 1968), p. 85.

Chapter 3
The New Deal

1. Robert S. McElvaine, *The Depression and the New Deal: A History in Documents* (New York: Oxford University Press, 2000), p. 42.

2. Ibid., p. 48.

3. Franklin Roosevelt's Statement on the National Industrial Recovery Act, June 16, 1933. Franklin D. Roosevelt Presidential Library and Museum.
http://www.fdrlibrary.marist.edu/odnirast.html

4. Ibid.

5. T. H. Watkins, *The Great Depression: American in the 1930s* (New York: Little, Brown, and Company, 1993), p. 311.

Chapter 4
The End of the Great Depression

1. Robert S. McElvaine, *The Depression and the New Deal: A History in Documents* (New York: Oxford University Press, 2000), p. 53.

Chapter 4 FYI
Day of Infamy

1. *National Park Service, U.S. Department of the Interior: USS Arizona Memorial,*
http://www.nps.gov/usar/fact_sheet.html

Chapter 5
Why the Great Depression Was Important

1. Robert S. McElvaine, *The Depression and the New Deal: A History in Documents* (New York: Oxford University Press, 2000), p. 170.

2. Ibid., p. 171.

For Further Reading

For Young Adults

Brennan, Kristine. *The Stock Market Crash of 1929.* Philadelphia: Chelsea House Publishers, 2000.

Damon, Duane. *Headin' for Better Times: The Arts of the Great Depression.* Minneapolis, Minnesota: Lerner Publication Company, 2002.

Meltzer, Milton. *Brother, Can You Spare a Dime?* New York: Facts on File, 1991.

Nishi, Dennis. *Life in the Great Depression.* San Diego, California: Lucent Books, 1998.

Works Consulted

Allen, Frederick Lewis. *Since Yesterday: The 1930s in America.* New York: Harper and Row, 1968.

Beno, Mike, editor. *'When the Banks Closed, We Opened Our Hearts.'* Greendale, Wisconsin: Reminisce Books, 1999.

Bendiner, Robert. *Just Around the Corner.* New York: Harper and Row, 1967.

Chronicle of the 20th Century. Mount Kisco, New York: Chronicle Publications, 1987.

Congdon, Don, editor. *The Thirties: A Time to Remember.* New York: Simon and Schuster, 1962.

Goldston, Robert. *The Great Depression.* Indianapolis: The Bobbs-Merrill Company, Inc., 1968.

The Great Depression. Volume 1: The Great Shake-Up. The History Channel, 1998.

The Great Depression. Volume 2: Face the Music. The History Channel, 1998.

McElvaine, Robert S. *The Depression and the New Deal: A History in Documents.* New York: Oxford University Press, 2000.

McElvaine, Robert S. *The Great Depression.* New York: Times Books, 1984.

Uys, Errol Lincoln. *Riding the Rails: Teenagers on the Move During the Great Depression.* New York: TV Books, 1999.

Watkins, T. H. *The Great Depression: America in the 1930s.* Boston: Little, Brown and Company, 1993.

On The Internet

The Handbook of Texas Online: *Dust Bowl*
http://www.tsha.utexas.edu/handbook/online/articles/view/DD/ydd1.html

Franklin Roosevelt's Statement on the National Industrial Recovery Act. June 16, 1933
http://www.fdrlibrary.marist.edu

The Iconography of Hope: The 1939-1940 New York World's Fair
http://xroads.virginia.edu/~1930s/DISPLAY/39wf/front.htm

PBS: *Wonders of the World Databank: Skyscraper - Empire State Building*
http://www.pbs.org/wgbh/buildingbig/wonder/structure/empire_state.html

Eye Witness to History: *Attack at Pearl Harbor, 1941*
http://www.eyewitnesstohistory.com/pearl.htm

American Rhetoric: *Franklin Delano Roosevelt: Pearl Harbor Address to the Nation*
http://www.americanrhetoric.com/speeches/fdrpearlharbor.htm

Indiana University: *League of Nations Archive*
http://www.indiana.edu/~league/

National Geographic: *Remembering Pearl Harbor*
http://plasma.nationalgeographic.com/pearlharbor/

National Park Service, U.S. Department of the Interior: *USS Arizona Memorial*
http://www.nps.gov/usar/

Glossary

broker (BROH-kur)
a person who buys and sells stocks for his or her clients, receiving a commission on each transaction.

collateral (kuh-LA-tuh-rull)
something of value given to a lender until a loan is repaid.

conservation (kahn-sur-VAY-shun)
the care and preservation of natural resources.

depression (dih-PREH-shun)
a period marked by severe slowing of business activity, much unemployment, falling prices, and reduced salaries.

dirigible (DEER-uh-juh-b'l)
a large motorized gas-filled balloon, usually cigar-shaped, that can be steered and having a cabin below for passengers.

drought (DROUT)
a very long period of abnormally dry weather.

economic (ee-kuh-NOM-ik)
having to do with the production and distribution of wealth.

invest (in-VEST)
to put money into stocks and bonds in order to earn a profit.

migration (my-GRAY-shun)
movement from one point to another.

pensions (PEN-shuns)
regularly scheduled payments made to people for retirement, disability, or similar reasons.

recession (ree-SEH-shun)
a temporary decrease in business activity.

stock (STOK)
shares in a corporation.

tariff (TAIR-uff)
fee charged on goods imported from foreign countries.

technology (tek-NOL-uh-gee)
the application of knowledge to practical purposes.

Index